Furies

Rachel Spence

Templar Poetry

Published in 2016 by Templar Poetry

Fenelon House
Kingsbridge Terrace
58 Dale Road, Matlock, Derbyshire
DE4 3NB

www.templarpoetry.co.uk

ISBN 978-1-911132-09-7

Typeset by Pliny

Cover Design and Artwork by Templar Design

Printed in England

Acknowledgements

I would like to thank Laura Scott and Tista Austin for reading drafts of some of these poems, Michael Rosas Cobian for his constant support, and my teachers Mimi Khalvati, Michael Saunders and Emi Tull.

'Right to Choose' was shortlisted in the 2016 Bridport Poetry Prize.

For

Jack, Sue, Philippa and Robin

CONTENTS

OUTSIDE THE BAKERY

Saturday, 10am, the Street of the Cats.
Morning hammered thin by rain, paving stones
licked by bronze. Outside the bakery,
four ladies boneless as the loaves in their trollies,
tossing a recipe for meatballs through rusty air.
A man passes, his cheeks pouched with middle-age.
"Angelo!" calls a lady. "I saw your mamma yesterday.
Why do you never visit her?" Chastened, he bows
his head, taking his scolding from a woman
for whom St Mark's Square is as far as Paris, unaware
that fifty years ago his mother was the local beauty,
a Titian blonde in swing skirt and stilettos,
that the bread buyers hissed *"putana"*as she passed.

HARD CITY

Night has left me raw. Heart-stalked.
Betrayals aggravated by their minor nature.

I wake to silence damp with the canal's secrets.
A gull boomerangs across the sky's blue wing.

Fumbling to catch thoughts like dropped stitches,
I stumble out into a morning made snappish

by its own beauty. The neighbourhood hugging
her pigments like spells: ochre; madder; ultramarine.

In the water, palaces hang like prints in a darkroom;
everybody stunned by fishbowl stillness.

You should know this is a hard city.
Somewhere a shift in the wind

can set even the dogs sulking. The pull of the tide
make you plot against your familiar.

You'll turn blind in your dreams,
wake speaking in tongues, look up from the stove

to find your child swapped for another;
a renunciation you can't remember making.

FOR ISABEL

I wake to fear and a froth of birdsong,
the curtains swollen with underwater light,
the canal taut as a layer of cellophane.

A painter sends me lines she has written
in a language that I do not speak
knowing I have the root to hand.

Certain words reveal themselves like flowers,
others clasp their provenance bud-tight.
I map a course across the Mediterranean,

out-running my own demons in pursuit
of another woman's fantasy
as the sky thickens, poised for thunder

FUGITIVE

Daybreak, the cathedral of Torcello,
light skinning the darkness from the windows,
glass lending your blue the fugitive touch of water.

Imagine a cave at midnight in the core of the mountain,
that's how deep you've kernelled your migrant knowledge,
nomad wisdom.

I think you were here before time,
before the rivers mingled with the sea.
They say your seed was planted in Jerusalem,

an era when you could reach back into history
and touch its fulcrum as it makes that slow,
perplexing pivot from truth to legend.

(Had you known you'd never
have worn that old blue gown,
your sister's hand-me-down.)

Luke said it didn't matter,
just the two of you alone in that upstairs room
in the old city, in a time before bells.

Nothing of that survives,
his goal was never likeness,
it was witness.

He told you to raise one hand and point,
he never said he'd add the baby later,
just one more someone who couldn't say His name.

A caesura that lasts centuries, dismantles gods.
Until what is left is you and your brittle, golden doll:
She who points the way.

And now you're here, on the threshold
of a city also burdened by an excess of declensions,
your truth as fleeting as the sheen of your sister's gown.

RIGHT TO CHOOSE

Madonna of triangles: perfect V
of flesh above your breastbone,
pyramid of cloak carving diagonals
out of the vowel of black. In an era
when geometry seemed God's own arithmetic,
perspective set you free as a night swimmer.
Then Antonello turned you inwards;
he dusted you with lamp-black,
made you edgeless in an edgeless world.
You are L'Annunziata
but your raised hand announces
that your womb will stay empty
as the darkness streaming behind you,
centuries of women holding their starless breath.

ANTONELLO'S SONG

I was born in harbour light —
porous, transient.
No wonder Venice spoke to me.

But I had changed by then.
In Tuscany, I met Piero,
his Mary's face blank as her pregnant belly,
an inland light, made for the plainsong
of the Tuscan hills, depth not ruled
but sung, form made
and unmade, until the eye learns to let go
find unity
              in anklebone and column,
brow and archivolt.

I was too good a pupil.
Piero would have made an offering
to the tangible:
shine bouncing off a pearl,
a little sigh of pattern.

My model's face said otherwise.

I found her selling eggs,
cheek mapping shell,
all around us the hysteria of market
and this girl,
              still as the afternote of a bell.

In Italy, we've drawn God into being.
Vittoria comes from somewhere else,
a place where He cannot be shown,
as if her bones had cancelled themselves out.

VITTORIA'S SONG

Madonna, he was arrogant!
Here, where there's a painter
for every fisherman,
he thought I'd gone unnoticed.
(Those Bellini boys bought eggs
enough to feed the army *torta*
for a month.)
I sent them all away –
my face an architecture of the no,
he says…
but how could I resist that swallowing darkness
in a city where light has too many tenses
                    to be desired
illegible   but not illiterate

The cloak was mine, curfew-blue and soft
as my best hen when I lift her from the lay,
I saw the lapis though –
just looking at it made me want
                    to pray.
Nothing of that colour
                              ever came into our house.
Falling in love
                        like stepping through a door,
casting off from the shore.
If innocence is found in numbers, what of our hearts?
Asking him after weeks spent measuring
each other's passion
                              for distance

MARY, MARY, QUITE CONTRARY

I don't know what you want from me,
and don't say "nothing" – I've heard that before.

Nothing will come of nothing

His favourite sum,
the Ground Zero of virginity.

It's true, I kept myself tidy.

Perhaps I thought my prince would come.
But waiting games are dangerous,

travelling inwards, I entered His blue prairie,

a door marked Solitude,
a room called Bliss

HOW DOES YOUR GARDEN GROW?

Walled.
Locked.
Hortus Conclusus.

Interviewing Dayanita Singh, New Delhi 2012

Greeting me alone, in the doorway of her studio. Behind her on the table, books: Ondaatje, Sebald, Calvino. A photographer who sculpts her pictures out of words. "Don't call me an artist; I'm a bookmaker."

Images pouring through her hands like liquid metal. Dipsticks of light plumbing an oil-black corridor. Girl on a bed, bare legs skewed in adolescent anger, her skin a forcefield of longing.

"Is it a poem? A short story? A novella?"

No, it's a *pietà*.

Somewhere between the morning coffee and the fish she grilled as the sky wrung out its last drop of hot blue, D talked of going solo — her realisation that a room of your own is not enough when you have many selves, each demanding a conversation with the other, each clamouring for silence.

But I am looking at the tripwire tension in those teenage hips.

Go Away Closer.

OVERHEARD I

"If I hadn't been a dancer,
I would have been a nun."

Darci Kistler, prima ballerina

telling us that what we saw

                              night after night

was not a woman   offering herself up

but one   turning herself inward

guarding her stage like a *hortus conclusus*

reciting her steps like a catechism

counting each beat of her private audience

confessing herself to God or her daemon?

                              duet for one

OVERHEARD II

"If I hadn't been a politican
               I would have been
a dancer."

Liz Kendall, Labour MP, (August 2015)

FOR FRANCESCA WOODMAN (AFTER ADRIENNE RICH)

The fact of a doorframe
gave you something to hold on to

as you moved through the world skinless,
wearing your broken rooms like water.

You propped Euclid on your pillow,
turned your lens on his mute glass eyes,

finding infinity in fugitive corners,
pockets of grace in imprecise angles,

prowling those parched thresholds
like a cat seeking sunlight,

less narcissist than pilgrim child,
undressing the elements like dolls.

BADLANDS

"It's a size you can walk into." Agnes Martin

When I heard that you saw your paintings as thresholds,
I thought of the archways between Virgin and Angel,
as if love was something to pass through.

How grateful we are for strict lines,
thirsty for a grammar of desire,
fearful of that unholy, illiterate blue.

You said your grids were innocent as trees,
pure as our third eye, a way to see
not what you saw but its internal grace.

To me, your lines are holding cells
for rage, graphs for plotting a woman's silence,
jotting her most secret peregrinations,

ciphers for a landscape so dangerous
it can't be given shape:
original, sinless, nothing to confess.

Mary wanders.
Medea waits.
God bless.

FOR NASREEN

"A spider can only make a web but it makes it to perfection." Nasreen Mohamedi

I never met you but I think you rose with the dawn
and napped before sunset, then gathered yourself
for a night at your drawing board,

swirl of fan
beating out the memory
of birds landing on the Kihim coast,

flute notes tracing
the view through the bars
of a balcony

on a day without sunlight,
when there is nothing
to see, anyway.

I could write of your body's betrayal
but your long eyes slide sideways
of you as woman, solo,

but you gesture to a faith
in love and work.
Reduce. Reduce. Reduce.

SONG FOR A LOST GIRL

Watch her as she walks, hips true as bells,
the swing and sway of them sets windows
rattling, shakes the oldest trees, her face carved
with razor blades and all the blood kept somewhere else.
Someone warns her the body has a memory
but she is done remembering.
Every morning she makes her peace with what remains
after the dark has fed, grateful that leftovers
cannot be hungry, cleansing herself in the innocence
of sidewalks, takeaway coffee like a holy offering,
praise song of car horns honouring her,
their commuter priestess!
Watch her – if Rumi's right and wounds are
where the light comes in, she is all shimmer

CORTE SCONTA

Our hands clasped across the table;
a prayer of fingers, text of flesh,

wrestling need out of the mute oak.
It could be Paris, Dakar, ancient Rome.

We have built a pyramid of blame,
stacking fault with the precision of children.

The waiters drop their charm offensive;
the rose seller gives us a wide berth.

Certain of victory, Language slinks off.
Our world cropped to the theatre of cutlery.

And you take my hand. Silence ruptures.
A couple close to us starts to quarrel.

CHRISTMAS QUARREL

New Year's Day, Battersea Park,
trees gleaming under sleeves of frost.
So once you shone when I drew near,
love coming off you like static.
Now you're holed up in memory's lair,
gnawing at your wounds to keep them raw,
and I'm… above me, a sudden froth of green.
Parrots! Second generation now, but still
that lime-bright shade is marvellous
among our northern blues and greys.
Difficult not to see them as messengers,
come to spread the word that
anything is possible: peace in the Middle East,
a surfeit of pandas, sorry.

FURIES

A week that began
with my anger
at your failure
to provide
insulation

           the tail-end of Gertrude whistling under
           your clapped-out windows

Wednesday, we're at the British Museum
you're turning the lives of the Pharoahs
into stories of your childhood and I'm still
snarling

both of us deaf to a people
who preserved not only the bodies of their dead
but also their shadows

Friday night brings armistice

David Attenborough discovering the world's largest dinosaur

ferrous-red thighbone as big as a pony

Faced with a hundred million years ago

and Imogen hurling *craquelures* of rain
against the window

what can we do but reach for each other?

3am, I draw back the curtain
penitent moonmaid, milking light
for our shadow

LETTER FROM THE PELOPONNESE

A week now that I have been sealed
into the paperweight world of the sailboat.
Waking to light like a bird of prey –
poised, hovering, stealing
its skin from rock and water.

I glimpse you as if through a telescope.
A man for whom freedom is a watchword,
with all the vigilance that implies.
Both rogue and stray, less absent than elsewhere,
always on the edge of leaving.

You would hear holy songs in the goat bells;
sacred rhythms in the whirr of the cicadas.
When you play, your fingers weave prayer carpets
of sound out of shapes no-one else can see.
Your music has hollowed me to the language of the morning.

At home you ask for silence as if it were a hymn
so that our rooms are shrines to cussing engines,
birdsong, our voices plaiting through open doorways.
Invisible braids of daily, stubborn listening
that haunt the house long after we are gone.

BREAKFAST WITH PALESTRINA

Clouds on fast-forward
      after a night of gales,
headache-blue sky,
      one of us needing sex,
the other stillness.
      Thank god for a composer
who quarried vowels
      from Lazio's sandstone light,
membrane of sound,
      contracting, expanding,
uncanny wings spreading
      under the burden of weightlessness.
You feel the effort.
      Flight *en pointe.*
The rolled-gold leap
      of resurrection, beaten, wound
into wedding bands of song

NOTES

FUGITIVE
The mosaic of the Madonna and Child in the cathedral of Torcello, in the Venice lagoon, is based on an earlier model, known as a Hodgeteria — She who shows the way — that, legend has it, was painted by St Luke.

RIGHT TO CHOOSE / ANTONELLO'S SONG / VITTORIA'S SONG / MARY, MARY / HOW DOES YOUR GARDEN
This sequence was inspired by a painting entitled the Vergine Annunziata by the Sicilian artist Antonello da Messina (c1430 -1479). It hangs in Palazzo Abatellis, the Regional Gallery of Art in Palermo, Sicily.

INTERVIEWING DAYANITA SINGH, DELHI 2012
Dayanita Singh, b.1961 New Delhi, is an artist. Her medium is photography and the book is her primary form. Go Away Closer is the title of one of her books.

BADLANDS
Agnes Martin (1912-2004) was an American abstract artist who worked primarily with the grid.

FOR NASREEN
Born in Karachi, then India now Pakistan, in 1937, Nasreen Mohamedi was an abstract artist who worked in pencil and pen and ink. She died in 1990.

MARY, MARY, QUITE CONTRARY
The quotation, "Nothing will come of Nothing" comes from *King Lear* by William Shakespeare.